50 Seasonal October Dishes for Home

By: Kelly Johnson

Table of Contents

- Pumpkin Soup
- Roasted Butternut Squash
- Apple Crisp
- Pumpkin Spice Pancakes
- Stuffed Acorn Squash
- Caramelized Onion and Pumpkin Tart
- Slow Cooker Beef Stew
- Maple Glazed Salmon
- Baked Sweet Potatoes with Cinnamon
- Roasted Root Vegetables
- Butternut Squash Risotto
- Spaghetti Squash with Marinara Sauce
- Roasted Brussels Sprouts with Bacon
- Pumpkin Bread
- Chicken Pot Pie
- Harvest Salad with Apples and Pecans
- Autumn Chili
- Apple Cider Glazed Pork Chops
- Pear and Gorgonzola Salad
- Roasted Chicken with Herbs
- Caramel Apple Cheesecake
- Pumpkin Ravioli
- Squash and Sage Risotto
- Baked Apple Cider Donuts
- Cinnamon Roasted Nuts
- Mushroom and Spinach Stuffed Chicken
- Spiced Carrot Cake
- Beef and Pumpkin Chili
- Pear and Prosciutto Pizza
- Pumpkin Curry Soup
- Roasted Chestnuts
- Sweet Potato Casserole
- Cranberry Sauce
- Sweet Potato Hash
- Autumn Vegetable Soup
- Pork Tenderloin with Apple Sauce

- Spicy Squash and Black Bean Enchiladas
- Cranberry Apple Crisp
- Pumpkin and Feta Salad
- Maple and Pecan Roasted Squash
- Pork and Apple Sausages
- Pumpkin Smoothie
- Harvest Shepherd's Pie
- Roasted Beet Salad with Goat Cheese
- Apple and Cheddar Grilled Cheese
- Caramelized Onion and Apple Gravy
- Cinnamon Streusel Coffee Cake
- Roasted Garlic and Pumpkin Hummus
- Apple and Sausage Stuffing
- Pecan Pie

Pumpkin Soup

Ingredients:

- 2 tbsp olive oil
- 1 medium onion, chopped
- 3 garlic cloves, minced
- 4 cups pumpkin puree (or roasted, blended pumpkin)
- 4 cups vegetable broth
- 1/2 tsp ground nutmeg
- Salt and pepper, to taste
- 1/2 cup heavy cream (optional)

Instructions:

1. In a large pot, heat olive oil over medium heat. Sauté the onion until soft (about 5 minutes), then add garlic and cook for another minute.
2. Stir in the pumpkin puree and vegetable broth.
3. Season with nutmeg, salt, and pepper.
4. Bring the mixture to a simmer and let cook for 15 minutes.
5. If you prefer a smooth texture, blend the soup using an immersion blender.
6. Stir in heavy cream if using, heat through, and serve warm.

Roasted Butternut Squash

Ingredients:

- 1 medium butternut squash, peeled and cubed
- 2 tbsp olive oil
- Salt and pepper, to taste
- 1/2 tsp dried thyme or rosemary (optional)
- 1-2 tsp maple syrup (optional, for a touch of sweetness)

Instructions:

1. Preheat your oven to 400°F (200°C).
2. Toss the butternut squash cubes with olive oil, salt, pepper, and herbs.
3. Spread evenly on a baking sheet and roast for 25–30 minutes until tender and lightly caramelized.
4. Drizzle with maple syrup if desired before serving.

Apple Crisp

Ingredients:

- 5-6 apples (Granny Smith or Honeycrisp), peeled, cored, and sliced
- 1 tbsp lemon juice
- 1/3 cup granulated sugar
- 1 tsp ground cinnamon
- 1/4 tsp ground nutmeg
- **For the topping:**
    - 3/4 cup old-fashioned oats
    - 1/2 cup all-purpose flour
    - 1/3 cup brown sugar
    - 1/2 tsp ground cinnamon
    - 1/4 cup cold butter, cut into small pieces

Instructions:

1. Preheat your oven to 350°F (175°C).
2. Toss apple slices with lemon juice, granulated sugar, cinnamon, and nutmeg. Spread evenly in a greased baking dish.
3. In a bowl, combine the oats, flour, brown sugar, and cinnamon. Cut in the butter until the mixture forms coarse crumbs.
4. Sprinkle the topping evenly over the apples.
5. Bake for 40–45 minutes until the apples are tender and the topping is golden brown.
6. Serve warm—ideally with a scoop of vanilla ice cream.

Pumpkin Spice Pancakes

Ingredients:

- 1 1/2 cups all-purpose flour
- 2 tbsp granulated sugar
- 2 tsp baking powder
- 1/2 tsp salt
- 1 tsp pumpkin spice blend (or 1/2 tsp cinnamon, 1/4 tsp nutmeg, 1/4 tsp ginger, pinch of cloves)
- 1 cup pumpkin puree
- 1 cup milk
- 1 egg
- 2 tbsp melted butter or oil
- 1 tsp vanilla extract

Instructions:

1. In a large bowl, whisk together flour, sugar, baking powder, salt, and pumpkin spice.
2. In another bowl, combine pumpkin puree, milk, egg, melted butter, and vanilla extract.
3. Pour the wet ingredients into the dry and stir until just combined (a few lumps are fine).
4. Heat a lightly oiled griddle or skillet over medium heat.
5. Pour 1/4 cup of batter for each pancake; cook until bubbles form on the surface, then flip and cook until golden brown.
6. Serve warm with maple syrup or your favorite toppings.

Stuffed Acorn Squash

Ingredients:

- 2 acorn squash, halved and seeded
- 2 tbsp olive oil
- Salt and pepper, to taste
- **For the filling:**
    - 1 cup cooked quinoa (or rice)
    - 1/2 cup dried cranberries
    - 1/2 cup chopped walnuts or pecans
    - 1 small apple, diced (optional)
    - 1 tsp ground cinnamon
    - 1 tbsp maple syrup
    - Fresh herbs (parsley or sage), chopped

Instructions:

1. Preheat oven to 400°F (200°C).
2. Brush the cut sides of the squash with olive oil, season with salt and pepper, and place cut-side down on a baking sheet.
3. Roast for about 30–35 minutes until tender.
4. Meanwhile, in a bowl, mix the quinoa with cranberries, nuts, apple, cinnamon, maple syrup, and herbs.
5. Once the squash is cool enough to handle, fill each half with the quinoa mixture.
6. Return to the oven for 5–10 minutes to warm the filling, then serve.

Caramelized Onion and Pumpkin Tart

Ingredients:

- 1 sheet puff pastry (thawed) or pie crust
- 2 cups pumpkin puree
- 2 large onions, thinly sliced
- 2 tbsp olive oil or butter
- 1 tsp fresh thyme leaves (or 1/2 tsp dried)
- Salt and pepper, to taste
- 1/2 cup crumbled goat cheese or feta (optional)

Instructions:

1. Preheat oven to 400°F (200°C).
2. In a skillet, heat olive oil or butter over medium-low heat. Add sliced onions with a pinch of salt and cook slowly until they are deeply caramelized (about 20–25 minutes).
3. Roll out the puff pastry on a baking sheet. Spread the pumpkin puree over the pastry, leaving a small border.
4. Distribute the caramelized onions evenly over the pumpkin puree. Sprinkle thyme, salt, pepper, and goat cheese if using.
5. Bake for 20–25 minutes until the pastry is golden and crisp.
6. Slice and serve warm or at room temperature.

Slow Cooker Beef Stew

Ingredients:

- 2 lbs beef stew meat, cut into cubes
- 3 carrots, cut into chunks
- 3 potatoes, peeled and cubed
- 1 large onion, chopped
- 3 cloves garlic, minced
- 4 cups beef broth
- 2 tbsp tomato paste
- 1 tsp dried thyme
- 1 bay leaf
- Salt and pepper, to taste
- 2 tbsp flour (optional, for thickening)

Instructions:

1. (Optional) Brown the beef in a skillet with a little oil for extra flavor before adding to the slow cooker.
2. Place beef, carrots, potatoes, onion, and garlic into the slow cooker.
3. Stir in beef broth, tomato paste, thyme, bay leaf, salt, and pepper.
4. Cover and cook on low for 7–8 hours (or on high for 4–5 hours) until the beef is tender.
5. If you prefer a thicker stew, mix the flour with a small amount of water to make a slurry and stir it in 15 minutes before serving.
6. Remove the bay leaf, adjust seasoning, and serve hot.

Maple Glazed Salmon

Ingredients:

- 4 salmon fillets
- 1/4 cup maple syrup
- 2 tbsp Dijon mustard
- 1 tbsp soy sauce
- 2 garlic cloves, minced
- Salt and pepper, to taste
- 1 tbsp olive oil

Instructions:

1. Preheat oven to 400°F (200°C).
2. In a small bowl, whisk together maple syrup, Dijon mustard, soy sauce, garlic, salt, and pepper.
3. Place salmon fillets on a lined baking sheet. Brush each fillet with olive oil and then generously coat with the maple glaze.
4. Bake for 12–15 minutes until the salmon flakes easily with a fork.
5. Serve immediately with a side of steamed vegetables or rice.

Baked Sweet Potatoes with Cinnamon

Ingredients:

- 4 medium sweet potatoes
- 1-2 tbsp olive oil
- Salt, to taste
- 1/2 tsp ground cinnamon
- 2 tbsp butter
- 1-2 tsp honey (optional)

Instructions:

1. Preheat oven to 400°F (200°C).
2. Wash and prick the sweet potatoes all over with a fork. Rub each with olive oil and a sprinkle of salt.
3. Place on a baking sheet and bake for 45–60 minutes, until tender when pierced with a fork.
4. Split open each sweet potato, add a pat of butter, sprinkle with cinnamon, and drizzle with honey if desired.
5. Serve warm.

Roasted Root Vegetables

Ingredients:

- 4 medium carrots, peeled and cut into 1-inch pieces
- 3 parsnips, peeled and cut into 1-inch pieces
- 2 medium sweet potatoes, peeled and cubed
- 2 tbsp olive oil
- 1 tsp dried rosemary
- 1/2 tsp garlic powder
- Salt and pepper, to taste

Instructions:

1. Preheat oven to 425°F (220°C).
2. Toss the carrots, parsnips, and sweet potatoes with olive oil, rosemary, garlic powder, salt, and pepper.
3. Spread the vegetables in a single layer on a baking sheet.
4. Roast for 25–30 minutes, stirring halfway through, until tender and lightly browned.
5. Serve warm.

Butternut Squash Risotto

Ingredients:

- 1 medium butternut squash, peeled and cubed
- 1 tbsp olive oil
- 1 medium onion, chopped
- 2 cups Arborio rice
- 1/2 cup dry white wine
- 4 cups chicken or vegetable broth, warmed
- 1/2 cup grated Parmesan cheese
- 2 tbsp butter
- Salt and pepper, to taste

Instructions:

1. Preheat oven to 400°F (200°C). Toss the cubed butternut squash with olive oil, salt, and pepper. Roast for 25 minutes until tender.
2. In a large saucepan, sauté the onion in olive oil until soft, about 5 minutes.
3. Add Arborio rice and cook, stirring for 1-2 minutes.
4. Pour in the white wine and stir until absorbed.
5. Gradually add the warmed broth, 1/2 cup at a time, stirring constantly, allowing the liquid to absorb before adding more.
6. Continue adding broth and stirring for about 20-25 minutes until the rice is creamy and tender.
7. Stir in the roasted butternut squash, Parmesan, and butter.
8. Season with salt and pepper and serve warm.

Spaghetti Squash with Marinara Sauce

Ingredients:

- 1 medium spaghetti squash
- 2 tbsp olive oil
- Salt and pepper, to taste
- 2 cups marinara sauce
- Fresh basil for garnish (optional)

Instructions:

1. Preheat oven to 400°F (200°C).
2. Cut the spaghetti squash in half lengthwise and scoop out the seeds.
3. Drizzle the cut sides with olive oil and season with salt and pepper.
4. Place the squash halves, cut side down, on a baking sheet and roast for 35-40 minutes, until tender.
5. Use a fork to scrape the flesh of the squash into spaghetti-like strands.
6. Warm the marinara sauce in a saucepan and pour over the spaghetti squash.
7. Garnish with fresh basil and serve.

Roasted Brussels Sprouts with Bacon

Ingredients:

- 1 lb Brussels sprouts, trimmed and halved
- 4 slices bacon, chopped
- 2 tbsp olive oil
- Salt and pepper, to taste
- 1 tbsp balsamic vinegar (optional)

Instructions:

1. Preheat oven to 400°F (200°C).
2. Toss the Brussels sprouts with olive oil, salt, and pepper.
3. Spread the Brussels sprouts on a baking sheet in a single layer.
4. Scatter chopped bacon over the sprouts.
5. Roast for 20-25 minutes, stirring halfway through, until the Brussels sprouts are crispy and browned.
6. Drizzle with balsamic vinegar if desired and serve warm.

Pumpkin Bread

Ingredients:

- 1 3/4 cups all-purpose flour
- 1 tsp baking soda
- 1/2 tsp salt
- 1 tsp ground cinnamon
- 1/2 tsp ground nutmeg
- 1/2 tsp ground ginger
- 2 large eggs
- 1 cup canned pumpkin puree
- 1/2 cup vegetable oil
- 1 cup granulated sugar
- 1/4 cup brown sugar
- 1 tsp vanilla extract

Instructions:

1. Preheat oven to 350°F (175°C). Grease a loaf pan.
2. In a bowl, whisk together flour, baking soda, salt, cinnamon, nutmeg, and ginger.
3. In a separate bowl, beat the eggs, pumpkin puree, oil, granulated sugar, brown sugar, and vanilla.
4. Gradually mix the dry ingredients into the wet ingredients until combined.
5. Pour the batter into the prepared loaf pan and bake for 60-70 minutes, until a toothpick inserted comes out clean.
6. Let cool before slicing.

Chicken Pot Pie

Ingredients:

- 2 cups cooked chicken, shredded
- 1 cup frozen peas and carrots
- 1/2 cup chopped onion
- 1/2 cup celery, chopped
- 3 tbsp butter
- 1/3 cup all-purpose flour
- 2 cups chicken broth
- 1/2 cup milk
- 1/2 tsp dried thyme
- Salt and pepper, to taste
- 1 package refrigerated pie crusts

Instructions:

1. Preheat oven to 375°F (190°C).
2. In a large saucepan, melt butter over medium heat and sauté onion and celery until soft.
3. Stir in flour and cook for 1-2 minutes.
4. Gradually add chicken broth and milk, stirring constantly until thickened.
5. Stir in cooked chicken, peas, carrots, thyme, salt, and pepper.
6. Roll out one pie crust and place it in a pie dish.
7. Pour the chicken mixture into the crust and top with the second crust.
8. Cut slits in the top crust and bake for 30-35 minutes, until golden brown.
9. Let cool for a few minutes before serving.

Harvest Salad with Apples and Pecans

Ingredients:

- 4 cups mixed greens (spinach, arugula, etc.)
- 1 apple, thinly sliced
- 1/2 cup candied pecans
- 1/4 cup crumbled goat cheese or feta
- 1/4 red onion, thinly sliced
- 1/4 cup balsamic vinaigrette

Instructions:

1. In a large bowl, combine the mixed greens, apple slices, pecans, goat cheese, and red onion.
2. Drizzle with balsamic vinaigrette and toss gently.
3. Serve immediately.

Autumn Chili

Ingredients:

- 1 lb ground turkey or beef
- 1 onion, chopped
- 2 cloves garlic, minced
- 1 can (15 oz) pumpkin puree
- 1 can (14.5 oz) diced tomatoes
- 1 can (15 oz) kidney beans, drained
- 1 can (15 oz) black beans, drained
- 1 tbsp chili powder
- 1 tsp ground cumin
- 1/2 tsp paprika
- Salt and pepper, to taste
- 1 cup chicken broth

Instructions:

1. In a large pot, brown the ground turkey or beef with onion and garlic over medium heat.
2. Stir in pumpkin puree, diced tomatoes, beans, chili powder, cumin, paprika, salt, and pepper.
3. Add chicken broth and bring to a simmer.
4. Let cook for 30 minutes, stirring occasionally.
5. Adjust seasoning as needed and serve warm.

Apple Cider Glazed Pork Chops

Ingredients:

- 4 pork chops
- 1 cup apple cider
- 1 tbsp Dijon mustard
- 1 tbsp brown sugar
- 1 tbsp apple cider vinegar
- 1 tbsp olive oil
- Salt and pepper, to taste

Instructions:

1. Season pork chops with salt and pepper.
2. In a large skillet, heat olive oil over medium-high heat. Brown the pork chops on both sides (about 3-4 minutes per side).
3. Remove pork chops and set aside.
4. In the same skillet, pour in apple cider, mustard, brown sugar, and apple cider vinegar. Bring to a simmer.
5. Return the pork chops to the skillet and cook for an additional 5-7 minutes, spooning the glaze over the chops.
6. Serve with the glaze spooned over the top.

Pear and Gorgonzola Salad

Ingredients:

- 4 cups mixed greens (arugula, spinach, or baby kale)
- 2 ripe pears, sliced
- 1/2 cup crumbled Gorgonzola cheese
- 1/4 cup toasted pecans or walnuts
- 1/4 red onion, thinly sliced
- 1/4 cup balsamic vinaigrette or pear vinaigrette

Instructions:

1. In a large bowl, toss the mixed greens, pear slices, Gorgonzola cheese, pecans, and red onion.
2. Drizzle with balsamic vinaigrette or pear vinaigrette and toss gently.
3. Serve immediately as a refreshing appetizer or side salad.

Roasted Chicken with Herbs

Ingredients:

- 1 whole chicken (about 4 lbs)
- 2 tbsp olive oil
- 1 lemon, quartered
- 4 garlic cloves, smashed
- 4 sprigs fresh rosemary
- 4 sprigs fresh thyme
- Salt and pepper, to taste

Instructions:

1. Preheat oven to 425°F (220°C).
2. Pat the chicken dry with paper towels and rub the skin with olive oil.
3. Stuff the cavity with lemon quarters, garlic, rosemary, and thyme.
4. Season the chicken generously with salt and pepper.
5. Place the chicken on a roasting rack in a roasting pan.
6. Roast for 1–1.5 hours, or until the internal temperature reaches 165°F (75°C) and the skin is golden and crispy.
7. Let the chicken rest for 10 minutes before carving and serving.

Caramel Apple Cheesecake

Ingredients:

- **For the crust:**
    - 1 1/2 cups graham cracker crumbs
    - 1/4 cup melted butter
    - 2 tbsp brown sugar
- **For the filling:**
    - 3 (8 oz) packages cream cheese, softened
    - 1 cup granulated sugar
    - 1 tsp vanilla extract
    - 3 large eggs
    - 1 cup sour cream
    - 2 tbsp all-purpose flour
- **For the topping:**
    - 2 apples, peeled and sliced
    - 1/2 cup caramel sauce
    - 1 tbsp butter
    - 1 tsp cinnamon

Instructions:

1. Preheat oven to 325°F (165°C).
2. Combine graham cracker crumbs, melted butter, and brown sugar. Press into the bottom of a springform pan.
3. Beat together cream cheese, sugar, vanilla, and flour until smooth. Add eggs one at a time, mixing well after each addition.
4. Pour the cheesecake filling over the crust.
5. Bake for 50-60 minutes, or until the center is set. Let cool to room temperature, then refrigerate for at least 4 hours.
6. In a skillet, sauté apples in butter with cinnamon until soft.
7. Drizzle caramel sauce over the cheesecake and top with the sautéed apples. Serve chilled.

Pumpkin Ravioli

Ingredients:

- 1 package fresh or frozen ravioli (filled with cheese or pumpkin)
- 1/2 cup canned pumpkin puree
- 1/4 cup heavy cream
- 2 tbsp butter
- 1/2 tsp ground sage
- Salt and pepper, to taste
- Fresh Parmesan cheese, for serving

Instructions:

1. Cook the ravioli according to package instructions.
2. In a saucepan, melt butter over medium heat. Add sage and cook for 1 minute.
3. Stir in pumpkin puree, heavy cream, salt, and pepper. Simmer for 3-5 minutes.
4. Toss the cooked ravioli in the pumpkin sauce and serve with freshly grated Parmesan.

Squash and Sage Risotto

Ingredients:

- 1 tbsp olive oil
- 1 small onion, finely chopped
- 1 cup Arborio rice
- 1 1/2 cups roasted butternut squash (cubed)
- 4 cups chicken or vegetable broth, warmed
- 1/2 cup white wine
- 1/2 tsp ground sage
- 1/2 cup grated Parmesan cheese
- 2 tbsp butter
- Salt and pepper, to taste

Instructions:

1. Heat olive oil in a large saucepan over medium heat. Add onion and sauté until softened.
2. Stir in Arborio rice and cook for 1–2 minutes.
3. Add the white wine and stir until absorbed.
4. Gradually add warm broth, 1/2 cup at a time, stirring constantly, until the rice is creamy and tender (about 20-25 minutes).
5. Stir in roasted butternut squash, sage, Parmesan cheese, butter, salt, and pepper.
6. Serve warm.

Baked Apple Cider Donuts

Ingredients:

- 1 1/2 cups all-purpose flour
- 1/2 tsp baking powder
- 1/2 tsp baking soda
- 1/4 tsp ground cinnamon
- 1/4 tsp ground nutmeg
- 1/4 tsp salt
- 1/4 cup brown sugar
- 1/2 cup apple cider
- 1/4 cup milk
- 1/4 cup unsalted butter, melted
- 1 large egg
- 1 tsp vanilla extract

Instructions:

1. Preheat oven to 350°F (175°C). Grease a donut pan.
2. In a bowl, whisk together the dry ingredients.
3. In another bowl, mix the wet ingredients.
4. Pour the wet ingredients into the dry ingredients and stir until just combined.
5. Spoon the batter into the donut pan.
6. Bake for 12–15 minutes or until a toothpick comes out clean.
7. Let the donuts cool for 5 minutes before transferring to a wire rack. Optionally, roll in cinnamon sugar for added flavor.

Cinnamon Roasted Nuts

Ingredients:

- 1 cup mixed nuts (walnuts, almonds, pecans, cashews)
- 2 tbsp honey
- 1 tbsp olive oil
- 1/2 tsp ground cinnamon
- 1/4 tsp salt

Instructions:

1. Preheat oven to 350°F (175°C).
2. In a bowl, toss the nuts with honey, olive oil, cinnamon, and salt.
3. Spread the nuts in a single layer on a baking sheet.
4. Roast for 10-15 minutes, stirring once or twice, until golden and fragrant.
5. Let cool before serving.

Mushroom and Spinach Stuffed Chicken

Ingredients:

- 4 boneless, skinless chicken breasts
- 1 cup fresh mushrooms, chopped
- 2 cups fresh spinach, chopped
- 1/2 cup cream cheese, softened
- 1/2 tsp garlic powder
- 1/4 tsp salt
- 1/4 tsp pepper
- 1 tbsp olive oil

Instructions:

1. Preheat oven to 375°F (190°C).
2. In a skillet, sauté mushrooms and spinach until softened, about 5 minutes.
3. Stir in cream cheese, garlic powder, salt, and pepper.
4. Cut a pocket in each chicken breast and stuff with the mushroom and spinach mixture.
5. Heat olive oil in a skillet and sear each chicken breast for 2-3 minutes per side.
6. Transfer the chicken to the oven and bake for 20-25 minutes until fully cooked.
7. Serve warm.

Spiced Carrot Cake

Ingredients:

- **For the cake:**
    - 2 cups all-purpose flour
    - 2 tsp baking powder
    - 1 1/2 tsp ground cinnamon
    - 1/2 tsp ground nutmeg
    - 1/2 tsp salt
    - 4 large eggs
    - 1 1/2 cups vegetable oil
    - 2 cups granulated sugar
    - 3 cups grated carrots
- **For the frosting:**
    - 8 oz cream cheese, softened
    - 1/4 cup unsalted butter, softened
    - 2 cups powdered sugar
    - 1 tsp vanilla extract

Instructions:

1. Preheat oven to 350°F (175°C). Grease and flour two 9-inch cake pans.
2. In a bowl, whisk together flour, baking powder, cinnamon, nutmeg, and salt.
3. In a separate bowl, beat eggs, oil, and sugar until smooth. Add grated carrots and mix well.
4. Gradually add the dry ingredients to the wet mixture and stir until combined.
5. Divide the batter between the two cake pans and bake for 25-30 minutes, until a toothpick comes out clean.
6. For the frosting, beat together cream cheese, butter, powdered sugar, and vanilla until smooth.
7. Once the cake has cooled, frost the layers and serve.

Beef and Pumpkin Chili

Ingredients:

- 1 lb ground beef
- 1 onion, chopped
- 2 cloves garlic, minced
- 1 can (15 oz) pumpkin puree
- 1 can (15 oz) diced tomatoes
- 1 can (15 oz) kidney beans, drained
- 1 can (15 oz) black beans, drained
- 1 tbsp chili powder
- 1 tsp cumin
- 1/2 tsp smoked paprika
- 1 cup beef broth
- Salt and pepper, to taste
- 1 tbsp olive oil

Instructions:

1. In a large pot, heat olive oil over medium heat. Brown the ground beef with onion and garlic.
2. Add the chili powder, cumin, smoked paprika, salt, and pepper. Stir to combine.
3. Stir in the pumpkin puree, diced tomatoes, kidney beans, black beans, and beef broth.
4. Bring to a simmer and cook for 30-40 minutes, stirring occasionally.
5. Adjust seasoning if needed and serve hot.

Pear and Prosciutto Pizza

Ingredients:

- 1 pizza dough (store-bought or homemade)
- 2 ripe pears, thinly sliced
- 4 oz prosciutto, thinly sliced
- 1/2 cup crumbled blue cheese or Gorgonzola
- 1/2 cup shredded mozzarella cheese
- 1 tbsp olive oil
- 1 tsp fresh thyme leaves
- Honey for drizzling (optional)

Instructions:

1. Preheat oven to 475°F (245°C).
2. Roll out the pizza dough onto a baking sheet or pizza stone.
3. Brush the dough with olive oil.
4. Layer with pears, prosciutto, blue cheese, and mozzarella.
5. Sprinkle with fresh thyme leaves.
6. Bake for 10-12 minutes, until the crust is golden and the cheese is melted.
7. Drizzle with honey (optional) before serving.

Pumpkin Curry Soup

Ingredients:

- 1 tbsp olive oil
- 1 onion, chopped
- 2 cloves garlic, minced
- 1 tbsp fresh ginger, grated
- 2 tbsp curry powder
- 1 can (15 oz) pumpkin puree
- 4 cups vegetable broth
- 1 can (13 oz) coconut milk
- 1/2 tsp salt
- 1/4 tsp ground cinnamon
- Fresh cilantro for garnish (optional)

Instructions:

1. In a large pot, heat olive oil over medium heat. Sauté the onion, garlic, and ginger for 5 minutes, until softened.
2. Stir in curry powder and cook for 1 minute.
3. Add the pumpkin puree, vegetable broth, coconut milk, salt, and cinnamon.
4. Bring to a simmer and cook for 20-25 minutes.
5. Use an immersion blender to puree the soup until smooth.
6. Garnish with fresh cilantro and serve warm.

Roasted Chestnuts

Ingredients:

- 1 lb chestnuts, scored
- 1 tbsp olive oil
- Salt, to taste

Instructions:

1. Preheat oven to 400°F (200°C).
2. Using a sharp knife, score an "X" on the flat side of each chestnut.
3. Toss the chestnuts with olive oil and salt.
4. Place on a baking sheet in a single layer.
5. Roast for 20-25 minutes, shaking the pan halfway through, until the shells open and the chestnuts are tender.
6. Peel the chestnuts while still warm and enjoy!

Sweet Potato Casserole

Ingredients:

- 4 medium sweet potatoes, peeled and cubed
- 1/4 cup unsalted butter
- 1/2 cup brown sugar
- 1/2 tsp ground cinnamon
- 1/4 tsp ground nutmeg
- 1/2 tsp vanilla extract
- 2 eggs, beaten
- 1/4 cup milk
- 1 cup mini marshmallows (optional)

Instructions:

1. Preheat oven to 350°F (175°C).
2. Boil the sweet potatoes in a pot of water for 15-20 minutes, until soft. Drain and mash.
3. Stir in butter, brown sugar, cinnamon, nutmeg, vanilla, eggs, and milk until well combined.
4. Transfer to a greased baking dish and smooth the top.
5. Top with marshmallows (optional) and bake for 25 minutes, until golden and bubbly.
6. Let cool slightly before serving.

Cranberry Sauce

Ingredients:

- 12 oz fresh cranberries
- 1 cup water
- 1 cup granulated sugar
- 1/4 cup orange juice
- Zest of 1 orange

Instructions:

1. In a saucepan, combine cranberries, water, sugar, and orange juice.
2. Bring to a boil, then reduce to a simmer.
3. Cook for 10-15 minutes, until the cranberries burst and the sauce thickens.
4. Stir in orange zest.
5. Let cool before serving.

Sweet Potato Hash

Ingredients:

- 2 medium sweet potatoes, peeled and diced
- 1 red bell pepper, chopped
- 1 onion, chopped
- 1 tbsp olive oil
- 1 tsp smoked paprika
- 1/2 tsp ground cumin
- Salt and pepper, to taste
- Fresh cilantro for garnish (optional)

Instructions:

1. Heat olive oil in a large skillet over medium heat.
2. Add the sweet potatoes and cook for 10-12 minutes, until tender.
3. Add the bell pepper and onion and cook for an additional 5 minutes, until softened.
4. Sprinkle with smoked paprika, cumin, salt, and pepper.
5. Garnish with fresh cilantro and serve.

Autumn Vegetable Soup

Ingredients:

- 1 tbsp olive oil
- 1 onion, chopped
- 2 carrots, chopped
- 2 celery stalks, chopped
- 2 potatoes, peeled and diced
- 1 zucchini, chopped
- 1 can (15 oz) diced tomatoes
- 4 cups vegetable broth
- 1 tsp dried thyme
- Salt and pepper, to taste

Instructions:

1. Heat olive oil in a large pot over medium heat. Add onion, carrots, and celery and cook for 5 minutes.
2. Stir in potatoes, zucchini, tomatoes, broth, thyme, salt, and pepper.
3. Bring to a boil, then reduce heat and simmer for 25-30 minutes, until vegetables are tender.
4. Adjust seasoning as needed and serve warm.

Pork Tenderloin with Apple Sauce

Ingredients:

- 2 pork tenderloins (about 1 lb each)
- 1 tbsp olive oil
- Salt and pepper, to taste
- 2 apples, peeled and sliced
- 1/4 cup apple cider or apple juice
- 1 tbsp brown sugar
- 1/2 tsp ground cinnamon
- 1/4 tsp ground nutmeg

Instructions:

1. Preheat oven to 375°F (190°C).
2. Season the pork tenderloins with salt and pepper.
3. Heat olive oil in an oven-safe skillet over medium-high heat. Sear the pork on all sides until browned, about 5 minutes.
4. Transfer the skillet to the oven and roast for 20-25 minutes, until the internal temperature reaches 145°F (63°C).
5. In a separate saucepan, combine apples, cider, brown sugar, cinnamon, and nutmeg. Cook over medium heat for 10-15 minutes until the apples are tender.
6. Serve the pork tenderloin with the apple sauce on top.

Spicy Squash and Black Bean Enchiladas

Ingredients:

- 2 cups roasted butternut squash, mashed
- 1 can (15 oz) black beans, drained and rinsed
- 1 tsp cumin
- 1/2 tsp chili powder
- 1/4 tsp cayenne pepper (optional, for extra heat)
- 1/2 cup red onion, chopped
- 2 cups enchilada sauce
- 8 corn tortillas
- 1 1/2 cups shredded cheddar or Mexican cheese
- 1 tbsp olive oil
- Salt and pepper, to taste

Instructions:

1. Preheat oven to 375°F (190°C).
2. In a bowl, combine the mashed butternut squash, black beans, cumin, chili powder, cayenne (if using), red onion, salt, and pepper.
3. Warm the tortillas slightly to make them pliable.
4. Spoon a portion of the squash and black bean mixture into each tortilla, roll it up, and place seam-side down in a baking dish.
5. Pour enchilada sauce over the rolled tortillas and sprinkle with shredded cheese.
6. Cover with foil and bake for 20 minutes.
7. Remove the foil and bake for an additional 5-10 minutes until the cheese is melted and bubbly.
8. Serve with sour cream or fresh cilantro, if desired.

Cranberry Apple Crisp

Ingredients:

- 2 cups fresh cranberries
- 2 apples, peeled, cored, and sliced
- 1/2 cup granulated sugar
- 1/2 tsp ground cinnamon
- 1/4 tsp ground nutmeg
- 1 tbsp lemon juice
- 1 cup old-fashioned oats
- 1/2 cup all-purpose flour
- 1/2 cup brown sugar
- 1/4 tsp salt
- 1/2 cup unsalted butter, cold and cubed

Instructions:

1. Preheat oven to 350°F (175°C).
2. In a bowl, toss the cranberries, apples, granulated sugar, cinnamon, nutmeg, and lemon juice. Transfer to a greased 9x9-inch baking dish.
3. In another bowl, mix oats, flour, brown sugar, and salt. Cut in the cold butter until the mixture resembles coarse crumbs.
4. Sprinkle the oat mixture evenly over the fruit.
5. Bake for 40-45 minutes, until the topping is golden brown and the fruit is bubbling.
6. Let cool slightly before serving with vanilla ice cream or whipped cream.

Pumpkin and Feta Salad

Ingredients:

- 2 cups mixed greens (arugula, spinach, or baby kale)
- 1 cup roasted pumpkin cubes
- 1/4 cup crumbled feta cheese
- 1/4 cup toasted pumpkin seeds
- 1/4 red onion, thinly sliced
- 2 tbsp olive oil
- 1 tbsp balsamic vinegar
- Salt and pepper, to taste

Instructions:

1. In a large bowl, combine the mixed greens, roasted pumpkin, feta, pumpkin seeds, and red onion.
2. In a small bowl, whisk together the olive oil, balsamic vinegar, salt, and pepper.
3. Drizzle the dressing over the salad and toss gently.
4. Serve immediately as a refreshing side or light main dish.

Maple and Pecan Roasted Squash

Ingredients:

- 1 medium butternut squash, peeled and cubed
- 1/4 cup maple syrup
- 1/4 cup olive oil
- 1/2 tsp ground cinnamon
- 1/4 tsp ground nutmeg
- 1/2 cup pecans, chopped
- Salt and pepper, to taste

Instructions:

1. Preheat oven to 400°F (200°C).
2. In a large bowl, toss the cubed squash with maple syrup, olive oil, cinnamon, nutmeg, salt, and pepper.
3. Spread the squash in a single layer on a baking sheet.
4. Roast for 20 minutes, then toss the squash and sprinkle the chopped pecans on top.
5. Continue roasting for another 15-20 minutes, until the squash is tender and caramelized.
6. Serve warm as a side dish.

Pork and Apple Sausages

Ingredients:

- 1 lb ground pork
- 1 apple, peeled and grated
- 1/4 cup breadcrumbs
- 1/4 tsp ground cinnamon
- 1/2 tsp ground sage
- 1/2 tsp garlic powder
- Salt and pepper, to taste
- 1 tbsp olive oil (for frying)

Instructions:

1. In a bowl, combine ground pork, grated apple, breadcrumbs, cinnamon, sage, garlic powder, salt, and pepper.
2. Form the mixture into sausage patties.
3. Heat olive oil in a skillet over medium heat.
4. Cook the sausage patties for 4-5 minutes per side, until golden brown and cooked through.
5. Serve with a side of roasted vegetables or on a bun with your favorite condiments.

Pumpkin Smoothie

Ingredients:

- 1/2 cup pumpkin puree
- 1/2 cup Greek yogurt
- 1/2 cup milk (or almond milk)
- 1/2 tsp ground cinnamon
- 1/4 tsp ground nutmeg
- 1 tbsp honey or maple syrup
- 1/2 tsp vanilla extract
- Ice cubes (optional)

Instructions:

1. In a blender, combine the pumpkin puree, Greek yogurt, milk, cinnamon, nutmeg, honey, and vanilla extract.
2. Blend until smooth.
3. Add ice cubes for a thicker texture if desired.
4. Serve chilled and enjoy!

Harvest Shepherd's Pie

Ingredients:

- 1 lb ground beef or lamb
- 1 onion, chopped
- 2 carrots, chopped
- 2 celery stalks, chopped
- 1 cup frozen peas
- 2 cups mashed potatoes
- 1/2 cup beef broth
- 2 tbsp tomato paste
- 1 tbsp Worcestershire sauce
- 1 tsp thyme
- Salt and pepper, to taste

Instructions:

1. Preheat oven to 375°F (190°C).
2. In a large skillet, cook the ground meat over medium heat until browned.
3. Add onion, carrots, and celery, cooking for another 5-7 minutes, until the vegetables are soft.
4. Stir in peas, tomato paste, Worcestershire sauce, thyme, beef broth, salt, and pepper.
5. Pour the mixture into a baking dish and top with mashed potatoes.
6. Bake for 20 minutes, until the top is golden and the filling is bubbly.
7. Serve warm.

Roasted Beet Salad with Goat Cheese

Ingredients:

- 3 medium beets, peeled and sliced
- 1 tbsp olive oil
- Salt and pepper, to taste
- 4 cups mixed greens
- 1/4 cup crumbled goat cheese
- 1/4 cup candied pecans (optional)
- 2 tbsp balsamic vinegar

Instructions:

1. Preheat oven to 375°F (190°C).
2. Toss the sliced beets with olive oil, salt, and pepper.
3. Spread the beets on a baking sheet and roast for 30-35 minutes, until tender.
4. Arrange the roasted beets on a platter and top with mixed greens, goat cheese, and candied pecans.
5. Drizzle with balsamic vinegar and serve.

Apple and Cheddar Grilled Cheese

Ingredients:

- 4 slices whole wheat or white bread
- 4 slices sharp cheddar cheese
- 1 apple, thinly sliced
- 2 tbsp butter

Instructions:

1. Heat a skillet over medium heat.
2. Butter one side of each slice of bread.
3. Layer the non-buttered side of two slices with cheese and apple slices.
4. Top with the remaining bread slices, buttered side facing out.
5. Grill for 3-4 minutes per side, until the bread is golden brown and the cheese is melted.
6. Serve warm with a side of soup or salad.

Caramelized Onion and Apple Gravy

Ingredients:

- 1 onion, thinly sliced
- 1 apple, peeled and chopped
- 1 tbsp butter
- 1 cup chicken broth
- 1 tbsp flour
- 1 tsp fresh thyme leaves
- Salt and pepper, to taste

Instructions:

1. In a skillet, melt butter over medium heat.
2. Add the onions and cook for 10-15 minutes, stirring occasionally, until caramelized.
3. Add the chopped apple and thyme and cook for 5 more minutes.
4. Stir in the flour and cook for 1-2 minutes.
5. Gradually add the chicken broth, stirring constantly, and simmer for 5-7 minutes, until the gravy thickens.
6. Season with salt and pepper, and serve over roasted meats or mashed potatoes.

Cinnamon Streusel Coffee Cake

Ingredients:

- **For the cake:**
    - 2 cups all-purpose flour
    - 1 cup granulated sugar
    - 1 tsp baking powder
    - 1/2 tsp baking soda
    - 1/2 tsp salt
    - 1/2 tsp ground cinnamon
    - 1/2 cup unsalted butter, softened
    - 2 large eggs
    - 1 tsp vanilla extract
    - 1 cup sour cream
- **For the streusel topping:**
    - 1/2 cup all-purpose flour
    - 1/2 cup packed brown sugar
    - 1/4 cup unsalted butter, cold and cubed
    - 1 tsp ground cinnamon

Instructions:

1. Preheat oven to 350°F (175°C). Grease a 9-inch round or square baking pan.
2. In a medium bowl, whisk together flour, sugar, baking powder, baking soda, salt, and cinnamon.
3. In a separate large bowl, cream together butter and eggs until light and fluffy.
4. Add vanilla extract and sour cream, mixing until smooth.
5. Gradually add the dry ingredients to the wet ingredients, stirring until just combined.
6. In a small bowl, combine the streusel ingredients (flour, brown sugar, butter, and cinnamon). Using a fork or pastry cutter, work the butter into the dry ingredients until crumbly.
7. Pour half of the cake batter into the prepared pan, sprinkle with half of the streusel topping. Add the remaining batter and top with the remaining streusel.
8. Bake for 40-45 minutes, until a toothpick inserted into the center comes out clean.
9. Allow to cool for 10 minutes before serving.

Roasted Garlic and Pumpkin Hummus

Ingredients:

- 1 can (15 oz) chickpeas, drained and rinsed
- 1/2 cup pumpkin puree
- 1 head garlic
- 2 tbsp tahini
- 2 tbsp olive oil
- 1 tbsp lemon juice
- 1/2 tsp ground cumin
- Salt and pepper, to taste
- 2-3 tbsp water, as needed

Instructions:

1. Preheat the oven to 400°F (200°C). Cut the top off the garlic head and drizzle with olive oil. Wrap it in aluminum foil and roast for 30-35 minutes until soft and caramelized.
2. Once the garlic is done, squeeze out the roasted garlic cloves into a food processor.
3. Add chickpeas, pumpkin puree, tahini, lemon juice, cumin, salt, and pepper. Process until smooth.
4. Gradually add water until the hummus reaches your desired consistency.
5. Serve with pita chips or fresh veggies.

Apple and Sausage Stuffing

Ingredients:

- 1 lb sausage (pork or turkey), casings removed
- 1 medium onion, chopped
- 2 celery stalks, chopped
- 2 apples, peeled, cored, and chopped
- 1 tbsp fresh sage, chopped
- 1/2 tsp dried thyme
- 1/2 cup chicken broth
- 1/4 cup unsalted butter
- 8 cups cubed bread (preferably a day or two old)
- Salt and pepper, to taste

Instructions:

1. Preheat oven to 375°F (190°C).
2. In a large skillet, cook sausage over medium heat, breaking it up with a spoon, until browned and cooked through. Remove sausage and set aside.
3. In the same skillet, melt butter and sauté the onion, celery, and apples until softened, about 5-7 minutes.
4. Add sage, thyme, salt, and pepper, and cook for another minute.
5. Stir in the cooked sausage and chicken broth.
6. In a large mixing bowl, combine the bread cubes with the sausage mixture. Stir until well combined.
7. Transfer the stuffing to a greased baking dish. Cover with foil and bake for 30-35 minutes.
8. Remove foil and bake for an additional 10-15 minutes until the top is golden brown.

Pecan Pie

Ingredients:

- 1 1/2 cups pecan halves
- 3/4 cup corn syrup
- 1/2 cup granulated sugar
- 1/2 cup brown sugar, packed
- 1/4 cup unsalted butter, melted
- 3 large eggs, lightly beaten
- 1 1/2 tsp vanilla extract
- 1/4 tsp salt
- 1 9-inch pie crust (store-bought or homemade)

Instructions:

1. Preheat the oven to 350°F (175°C).
2. In a large bowl, whisk together corn syrup, granulated sugar, brown sugar, melted butter, eggs, vanilla extract, and salt.
3. Stir in the pecans.
4. Pour the mixture into the prepared pie crust.
5. Bake for 50-60 minutes, until the pie is set and golden brown on top (check after 30 minutes and cover with foil if the edges are getting too dark).
6. Allow the pie to cool completely before slicing and serving.